This Book Belongs to:

Consultant: Fiona Moss RE Adviser at RE Today Services
Editor: Cathy Jones
Designer: Chris Fraser

Copyright © QED Publishing 2012

First published in the UK in 2012 by
QED Publishing
A Quarto Group company
230 City Road
London EC1V 2TT

www.qed-publishing.co.uk

A catalogue record for this book is available
from the British Library.

ISBN 978 1 84835 896 6

Printed in China

Moses
in the
Bulrushes

Written by Katherine Sully
Illustrated by Simona Sanfilippo

QED Publishing

Once there was a girl called Miriam who lived in Egypt. Her family were Hebrew slaves.

There were many Hebrew slaves in Egypt working for the king.

One day, the king gave an order:
"There are enough Hebrews in Egypt.
There must be no more baby boys."

The king sent soldiers to
all the Hebrew villages.

If they found any baby boys,
they would kill them!

Miriam's mother had a baby boy.
"What are we to do?"
Miriam cried.

Miriam's mother hid the baby in the house and Miriam watched over him.

"Shh, little brother. Be good for Mother!"

But when the baby was three months old, he was
too big and too noisy to hide in the house any longer.

Miriam's mother found a basket and painted it so that it would not leak. Then she wrapped the baby in a blanket and put him in the basket.

When no one was looking, Miriam and her mother carried the basket down to the river and hid it among the bulrushes.

Miriam's mother hurried back to the house
leaving Miriam to watch the baby.
All day, Miriam hid nearby to make
sure the baby was safe.

"Shh, little brother.
Be good for Mother!"

Then, from her hiding place, Miriam could see some people coming.

The king's daughter was walking along the river bank with her servants.

She saw something floating in the bulrushes.
"Fetch that for me to see," she told
her servant.

The servant brought the little basket to the king's daughter. It floated just like a little boat! The king's daughter looked inside the basket . . .
. . . and was amazed.

"It's a baby boy!" she smiled.
The king's daughter lifted
the baby from the basket.

The baby began to cry.

Just then, Miriam jumped up
from her hiding place.

"Shall I fetch someone to feed
the baby and look after him
for you?" she asked.

"Yes, that's a good idea,"
said the king's daughter.

Miriam ran to find her mother and together they hurried down to the river.

"I will pay you money to feed this baby and look after him for me," said the king's daughter.

And she handed the baby to his mother.

Miriam and her mother were very happy.

They took the
baby back home
and cared for
him until he was
old enough to go
to the palace.

The king's daughter was delighted.
"I will bring him up like a son," she
smiled. "I will call him Moses."

Next Steps

Look back through the book to find more to talk about and join in with.

* Copy the actions. Be a little basket bobbing in the bulrushes.

* Join in with the rhyme. Pause to encourage joining in with 'Shh, little brother. Be good for Mother.'

* Counting. Count five birds, five butterflies, three slaves and three vases.

* Colourful flowers. Name the colours of the flowers by the river together, then look back to spot the colours on other pages.

* All shapes and sizes. Compare the basket and chest that Moses is hidden in as he grows.

* Listen to the sounds. When you see the word on the page, point and make the sound – Shh! Wah!

Now that you've read the story... what do you remember?

* Who was Moses?
* Why did his mother hide him in a basket?
* How old was Moses when he was taken to the river?
* Where did Miriam hide the basket?
* What happened when the king's daughter came to the river?
* When did Moses go to live at the palace?

What does the story tell us?
Sometimes our enemies can become our friends.